THE WOR IS HUSHED

BY KEITH BUNIN

DRAMATISTS
PLAY SERVICE
INC.

For everyone at Oakwood Friends School

THE BUSY WORLD IS HUSHED was developed at New York Stage & Film, the Ojai Playwrights Conference, and Madison Repertory Theatre.

THE BUSY WORLD IS HUSHED received its Off-Broadway premiere by Playwrights Horizons (Tim Sanford, Artistic Director; Leslie Marcus, Managing Director) on June 20, 2006. It was directed by Mark Brokaw; the set design was by Allen Moyer; the costume design was by Michael Krass; the lighting design was by Mary Louise Geiger; the original music was by Lewis Flinn; the production stage manager was David Sugarman; and the assistant stage manager was Mary Kathryn Flynt. The cast was as follows:

BRANDT .... Hamish Linklater
HANNAH .... Jill Clayburgh
THOMAS .... Luke Macfarlane

CHARACTERS

BRANDT

HANNAH

THOMAS

PLACE

The library of an apartment
on West 122nd Street, New York City.

TIME

The present.

ACT ONE
August to November.

ACT TWO
November to February.

THE BUSY WORLD IS HUSHED

ACT ONE

Scene 1

The library of an apartment on West 122nd Street in New York City. A warm Monday afternoon in August. A large wooden table sits in the middle of the room, surrounded by several mismatched old chairs. No shelves. Books are piled up everywhere, on and around the table and in stacks up against the walls and strewn all over the floor. Sliding doors on one wall lead to the front hall and an open portal opposite leads to the bedrooms. The back wall is dominated by large picture windows, including several ornate stained-glass windows which depict events in the life of Jesus. Outside the windows it is bright and sunny. The whole room gives off an inviting, friendly glow. Brandt, 30, sits nervously in one of the mismatched chairs. He is dressed nicely but somehow clothes don't fit comfortably on him. Hannah, 50s, dressed in a clerical collar and civilian clothes, stands behind the table holding a package.

BRANDT. Another gospel?

HANNAH. Arrived in my mailbox just this morning. A second-century Coptic translation from I'm guessing an Aramaic original that may very well have been composed as early as 50 or 60 A.D.

BRANDT. And it came UPS. *(Hannah picks up a letter opener and slices the package open.)*

HANNAH. Even better, it's a Xerox. The original is safe and sound in the Coptic Museum in Cairo. A bequest from an Egyptian billionaire whose family has secretly possessed it since the late 1800s, when one of their servants found it buried in a cave. Finally restored to the world after vanishing for nearly two thousand years.

BRANDT. And on my first day of work.

HANNAH. I don't believe you've been hired yet.

BRANDT. Aren't you supposed to walk into the interview like you've already got the job? Shouldn't I try to impress you with my initiative? *(Hannah puts on her glasses and picks up a folder from the table.)*

HANNAH. Tell me, what is your experience of the Episcopal Church?

BRANDT. I was baptized and confirmed at St. Luke's downtown.

HANNAH. Were you? Really? What was that like for you?

BRANDT. I made lots of vaguely Bible-related crafts out of felt.

HANNAH. The 1970s have a great deal to answer for.

BRANDT. What I remember most clearly is this one prayer. They'd say it every Sunday after the recessional. I'd be playing with the buttons on my dad's scratchy suit. *(Recites lightly from memory.)* "O Lord, support us all the day long, until the shadows lengthen and the evening comes, and the busy world is hushed … "

HANNAH. *(Nods, fondly.)* " … and the fever of life is over, and our work is done. Then in Thy mercy grant us a safe lodging, and a holy rest, and peace at the last."

BRANDT. It's so plain and so perfect. Even when I was ten I could see it's a benediction for the end of the day and the end of my days. *(Hannah appraises Brandt closely from behind her glasses.)* It's a prayer for the dutiful and the weary, and it doesn't ask God for power or glory, just comfort and safety. And it pretty clearly guarantees that whatever's waiting in the next life is as simple and as wonderful as a good night's sleep. *(A beat.)* It's the first piece of writing I truly, consciously loved. *(Hannah is silent for a moment. Then she leafs through the folder.)*

HANNAH. From what I see here, you're completely unqualified for this job.

BRANDT. *(Taken aback a moment.)* Am I? Really? That's too bad. Are you sure?

HANNAH. The book that I've been contracted to write is a translation and interpretation of this gospel. My assistant should be fluent in Coptic, Greek, and Aramaic. He should also have a firm grasp on the rivalries among all the factions of early Christianity.

BRANDT. I'm completely unqualified for this job.

HANNAH. Be that as it may. I have lean and hungry grad students who'd be more than happy to do the necessary grunt work. What I need is an excellent writer who can clarify my thoughts so they flow pleasingly on the page. Do you understand what's required here?

BRANDT. I think maybe you want me to write the book for you.

HANNAH. Not to put too fine a point on it, but yes. Talking is easy for me, as I'm sure you've already gathered. I give all my sermons and lectures completely extemporaneously. I can warn you, it's generally going to be impossible to shut me up.

BRANDT. I'll definitely keep that in mind.

HANNAH. But sit me down at a computer and my fingers freeze over the keyboard. Back at seminary I had to pay my roommate to write my sermons for me, otherwise I would've flunked out.

BRANDT. What a mind-blowing ethical and religious dilemma.

HANNAH. It's an awful thing, when you have something of value to impart but you have no idea how to make yourself clear.

BRANDT. I'm fairly sure I can help you with this. *(Hannah picks up a manuscript from the table and considers it.)*

HANNAH. Our mutual editor recommends you very highly.

BRANDT. Jason has always been really supportive of me.

HANNAH. He sent me a chapter of your Christina Rossetti biography, which I quite liked. I must admit I wasn't familiar with her work.

BRANDT. Almost nobody is. Lately it seems a little stupid, devoting all this energy to a book that maybe five people will read.

HANNAH. So what else is new? Every week I preach at the prison up in Beacon, where most of the inmates only come to chapel to get out of their cells for an hour. I give communion in the Alzheimer's ward at York Hospital. We always speak into a void, we never know if anyone is listening. And how is your book coming along?

BRANDT. Did you know eventually the sun is going to become a red giant? It'll swell to five times its size and swallow up the earth. Then it'll burn out and our solar system will be black and cold. A few weeks after that, I might conceivably have a workable first draft.

HANNAH. Is there anything in particular that's keeping you from finishing?

BRANDT. You're not really interested in this.

HANNAH. I certainly don't want a blocked writer for my assistant.

BRANDT. *(Extends his arms helplessly.)* One thing I've learned about life, it has a habit of intervening. *(Hannah considers Brandt carefully and steps a little closer to him.)*

HANNAH. Let's talk about logistics. We'd have to meet up at odd hours to work around my teaching schedule and my other commitments.

BRANDT. Honestly I'd just love to have someplace I need to go every day.

HANNAH. I'd expect you to do a lot of research on your own. You'd have a key to the apartment so you could make use of this library.

BRANDT. I have to admit I've got a huge crush on your library. Whenever you turn your head for a minute I'm speed-reading the spines of all your books. Plus I think it's really revolutionary to have a library with absolutely no bookshelves.

HANNAH. I'm afraid that's due to desperation rather than design. My son is supposed to be building new shelves for me but he's abdicated.

BRANDT. And these stained-glass windows are breathtaking.

HANNAH. I despise them with a passion. I'd smash them to bits if this wasn't subsidized faculty housing.

BRANDT. I'm just going to quit trying to impress you now.

HANNAH. (Getting surprisingly worked up.) They're everything I hate about what Christianity has become. A religion born from abject poverty in an occupied nation, twisted into such self-important nonsense. Look at this Annunciation: It's like Gabriel's come down for tea with the Princess of Monaco. (She gestures to the center window which depicts Mary and Jesus.) When really Mary was a frightened child with a terrifying responsibility. Certainly she was never this worriless mother playing with a perfect infant God who never cried. Forget that it's a travesty of Christianity: it's a mockery of motherhood. (The door flies open and Thomas, 26, barrels into the room, a knapsack on his back, face and body smudged with dirt and blood, the expression on his face completely exultant.)

THOMAS. First of all this is mostly not my own blood.

HANNAH. I have a horrible feeling that's meant to be reassuring.

THOMAS. I'm just saying there's no reason to fly off the handle.

HANNAH. This is my son with whom I am not pleased. (Brandt extends his hand to Thomas.)

THOMAS. I wouldn't shake my hand if I were you. There's dried crap all over it. I'm afraid most of that is mine. Long story.

HANNAH. Apparently you spent the last three days at the bottom of a ditch.

THOMAS. You know where I've been. I've been playing get lost. (Thomas pulls off his knapsack.)

10

BRANDT. I don't think I know that game.

HANNAH. One of my son's most hateful inventions. He came up with it when he was ten and I had my parish upstate. He'd ride off on his bike until night fell and his legs were aching and he didn't know where he was anymore. And then he'd have to find his way home.

THOMAS. I was teaching myself navigation and self-reliance.

HANNAH. You were also giving me roughly fifteen heart attacks every week.

THOMAS. That was just a nice bonus.

HANNAH. Now he's theoretically a grown-up, he's still playing get lost, only his stadium is the entire world.

THOMAS. *(Leans in to Brandt, conspiratorial.)* A gross exaggeration. I took Amtrak up to the Catskills. Hitched a ride with some trucker, dropped me off at the base of the trail. Only brought enough provisions for one day, to really kick my ass.

HANNAH. So it's just luck your entrails aren't being devoured by vultures.

THOMAS. Not too many vultures in the Catskills. Any entrail-devouring would have to be done by a passing family of backwoods cannibals.

BRANDT. But it's not really dangerous. My dad used to take me camping in the Catskills, that place is mapped out pretty comprehensively.

HANNAH. Of course you're assuming that Thomas brought a map with him.

THOMAS. A map totally defeats the purpose of playing get lost. I'd think that would be self-evident.

HANNAH. Now you see what I'm dealing with.

THOMAS. *(Leans in to Brandt, grinning.)* Believe it or not, I've only been back home for a month. It's going wonderfully well so far, don't you think?

BRANDT. You know you've got weird spiky things sticking out of your leg?

THOMAS. It isn't any big deal, see, I just got attacked by this dog.

HANNAH. Oh, Thomas, have you come home with rabies again?

BRANDT. Now there's a problem that's never come up in my family.

THOMAS. Last night I'm camping out, I hear these coyotes in the brush, they make this high-pitched squeal whenever they find a kill. And then I hear this sad little whimpering, it's unmistakably a puppy.

BRANDT. This isn't one of those happy nature stories, I can

11

already tell.

THOMAS. So I run into the bushes howling like a banshee and the coyotes scatter and this little puppy is sitting there shaking like a leaf and I reach out to pet him and he bites me really hard right here. *(With enormous pride, Thomas shows them the gash on his ankle.)*

BRANDT. That seems a little ungrateful.

THOMAS. Poor puppy's just traumatized. I hold him and rock him to sleep. And I figure I'm on a walkabout and this here is my animal guide.

HANNAH. Your animal guide would definitely almost get eaten by coyotes.

THOMAS. So I christen him Siddhartha. And this morning we're walking along and Siddhartha ambles off into the brush to pee when all of a sudden he lets out this bloodcurdling howl.

BRANDT. If the dog dies at the end of the story I'm gonna be so upset.

THOMAS. So I run into the brush and I see that Siddhartha has tons of these long spiky things sticking out all over his fur.

BRANDT. *(The light dawning.)* Those are porcupine quills stuck in your leg.

THOMAS. Whimpering like you've never seen, the depths of canine despair, I take hold of him and yank out the quills, and now he's bawling, the agony is unbearable, but finally I pull all the quills out.

BRANDT. He really is just about the worst possible animal guide.

THOMAS. Yeah, except it gets even worse. Because now I'm carrying Siddhartha in my arms, he's still weeping from the pain, when we turn the corner and there right in front of us is the porcupine.

BRANDT. Now you're just making stuff up.

THOMAS. I wish. Because Siddhartha leaps out of my arms and runs over to the porcupine … and licks her face! He just wants to be friendly. He hasn't learned a single thing.

HANNAH. He's a lot like someone in this room.

THOMAS. So now I go nuts, I drop-kick the porcupine into the brush. And the quills are stuck in Siddhartha's tongue so I pry open his mouth and pull them out with my teeth.

HANNAH. He does all this for a mangy puppy but I can't get him to build me some lousy bookshelves.

BRANDT. You've got to get those quills out of you.

THOMAS. They're my badge of honor. I'm never taking them out.

HANNAH. That's the most asinine thing I've ever heard.

THOMAS. These are my battle scars. They bind me forever to

Siddhartha, my brave and excellent animal guide.

BRANDT. You saw how much it hurt the puppy so now you're scared, it's only natural. But you'll get an infection if you don't take them out. I can do it, I worked in a vet's office all through high school. *(Hannah and Thomas consider Brandt. Then Thomas nods to him.)*

THOMAS. Do your worst.

BRANDT. Don't worry about it: This is barely going to hurt at all. *(Brandt kneels down at Thomas' feet and pulls out one of the quills.)*

THOMAS. *(With a yelp of pain.)* Oh, Jesus Christ, that was excruciating.

BRANDT. Yeah, I figured it would be, I was just trying to trick you there. Okay, now let's try some creative visualization. Close your eyes and pretend you're on a pink cloud in a sky made of candy when all of a sudden you feel a really sharp pain in your leg. *(Brandt pulls out another quill.)*

THOMAS. *(Laughing despite himself.)* Fuck, you have a hell of a bedside manner, you know that?

BRANDT. *(Very gently and tenderly.)* Why don't you finish the story? What happened to the dog? *(Brandt starts pulling the rest of the quills out. Hannah watches the two of them very closely.)*

THOMAS. *(Flinching slightly throughout.)* We're limping down the trail and we run into this park ranger. He tells us that a dog matching Siddhartha's description ran off from a campsite two weeks ago, and the family's been frantic, their little girl's been crying herself to sleep every night.

BRANDT. I just need you to stop bouncing your leg.

THOMAS. We get back to the ranger station and it turns out Siddhartha does belong to this little girl and his name is actually Fluffy.

BRANDT. How disappointingly prosaic.

THOMAS. I know, right? So the ranger takes Fluffy back to his family and I get on Amtrak and the One train uptown. One advantage to looking and smelling the way I do, you get almost a whole subway car to yourself even at rush hour. And now home to you.

BRANDT. And there you are: good as new. *(Rising, Brandt lets the quills tumble into the wastebasket. Thomas considers him closely.)*

HANNAH. So how exactly am I supposed to respond to all this?

THOMAS. You could be happy I saved that little girl's puppy.

HANNAH. Why are you trying to kill yourself?

THOMAS. Now you're really flying off the handle.

HANNAH. When you're older, you'll look back, and you'll realize you were trying to kill yourself. *(Thomas opens his mouth to respond, but then thinks better of it. He rises from his chair.)*

THOMAS. I should probably clean myself up.

HANNAH. And get some food in you. I have an interview to finish. *(Thomas nods. On his way out he turns and smiles at Brandt.)*

THOMAS. I hope we haven't scared you away. *(Thomas is gone. Hannah stares after him for a moment.)*

HANNAH. Now I've lost my train of thought.

BRANDT. I think you were about to offer me the job.

HANNAH. You can't possibly be so maddening to your parents.

BRANDT. Is there anything else you need to ask me? *(Hannah puts on her glasses, consulting the folder.)*

HANNAH. Just one more question: What's your relationship to Jesus Christ?

BRANDT. Are you sure you're allowed to ask me that?

HANNAH. Under the circumstances I think it's entirely relevant.

BRANDT. It's just a little complicated.

HANNAH. If you're concerned an honest answer might cost you this job, you should know I'm often inclined to hire agnostics as my assistants. It forces me to be rigorous: I speak far more clearly around people who aren't comfortable with my language.

BRANDT. You're an equal opportunity employer, then.

HANNAH. Every Sunday at Eucharist we say a prayer for those whose faith is known to God alone. I take that to mean the people who don't think God exists but who still behave in line with His wishes for them. If I were God, the last thing that would concern me about my children is whether or not they believed in me.

BRANDT. *(Takes a deep breath.)* First off, as a gay man, I find the church's attitude toward me personally at best queasily forbearing and at worst homicidal.

HANNAH. You'd be hard-pressed to find a single word from the historical Jesus that condemns homosexuality. Any unpleasant rhetoric of that nature has been entirely invented by frightened bigots who need to make demons of their fellow men because they're too cowardly to confront the demons within their own souls.

BRANDT. Impressive how you can decimate thousands of years of prejudice and persecution in a couple of sentences like that.

HANNAH. *(Smiles wryly at him.)* If only anyone would actually listen to me.

BRANDT. Plus I guess to be honest lately I've been struggling with the idea that maybe all religion is just a desperate attempt to make death more bearable. The dream that our loved ones are just waiting for us to join them on some distant shore.

HANNAH. Who is it that you've lost? *(She holds him in her steady gaze. He stuffs his hands in his pockets.)*

BRANDT. About a year ago my dad started having these seizures, which the doctors first thought were stress-related and then maybe heart-related, but in July somebody did a brain scan and it turns out there's a tumor wrapped around a few of his nerves.

HANNAH. I'm so very sorry.

BRANDT. *(Waves it away with his hand.)* Anyway at the moment we're in the thick of a series of tests to determine if the tumor will respond to radiation.

HANNAH. And how is your father handling all this?

BRANDT. He's stoic as always. But last weekend was especially brutal, so late Sunday night we had one of those awful conversations about worst-case scenarios, and even though he hasn't set foot in St. Luke's since I got confirmed he'd really like an Episcopal burial. *(As Hannah stares at him, her face slowly changes. Brandt toes the floorboards with his shoe.)* Which I'm afraid at this late date means some minister who barely knew him will be up at the altar with a few stories about his army medals and golf handicaps.

HANNAH. And is your mother all right with this decision?

BRANDT. Since my dad got diagnosed she's seeing angels everywhere. We walk through the park, she says, doesn't that cloud look just like an angel? Yesterday she brought me into the kitchen, she swears she can see the face of the Virgin Mary in the teak cabinets.

HANNAH. But understandably you find all of that less than convincing.

BRANDT. *(With tremendous simplicity.)* I do find it hard to square the idea of a benevolent all-powerful creator with the details of my daily life right now. I mean, it's relatively easy for Christianity to explain wars and genocides. Blame them on the Devil or a world gone wrong. *(Hannah sinks into a chair, watching Brandt very intently.)* But watching my father die is the most natural, inevitable thing. It's how the world is supposed to work and it's unspeakably cruel. *(Hannah takes off her glasses and closes the folder on her desk.)*

HANNAH. Twenty-seven years ago my husband drowned off the coast of Maine. I'm not trying to compare our situations. I just want you to know I'm not entirely without a frame of reference.

BRANDT. You don't have to do this.

HANNAH. Really I'd like to. One thing I can tell you from experience, even if you have no faith at all, a church can be a very useful place to visit. Because it's one of the few rooms in the world where terrible grief isn't unwelcome. And if you stay in the room long enough, you might actually receive some kind of answer.

BRANDT. *(Smiles slightly.)* Of course I'd like to believe that. I'd also like to believe that I'm six years old and I'm lying in the back seat of our Chevy Nova late at night and I can fall asleep knowing my father's in the driver's seat and he'll get us home safe and sound.

HANNAH. *(A moment, then, carefully:)* Do you worry it might not be a good time for you to take this job?

BRANDT. The thought did cross my mind.

HANNAH. But you still came in for the interview.

BRANDT. First off I'm very good at what I do. And I'm certain I can articulate your beliefs effectively, whether or not they coincide with the thoughts buzzing around my own brain.

HANNAH. I have no doubts about your abilities.

BRANDT. And as far as my father is concerned, it's not like the end is near, most likely there are years of torture yet to come, so I need to retain some semblance of a normal life.

HANNAH. Of course that's what you have to do.

BRANDT. But lately I'm finding it kind of impossible to get any of my own writing done, so frankly the best thing for me would be to take on a good job that'll get me out of my house and my head.

HANNAH. That makes a great deal of sense.

BRANDT. Yes, well, so even if I can't offer you my faith, I can definitely promise you my sweat and tears and total grateful devotion. *(Hannah considers. She opens a box and takes out a key ring.)*

HANNAH. This key gets you into the lobby, these two are for the apartment. I'll call Jason and tell him to draw up your contract.

BRANDT. Clearly I should throw myself on people's mercy more often.

HANNAH. A week working for me and you'll be expert at begging for mercy.

BRANDT. I guess it's too late for me to back out now.

HANNAH. *(Extends her arm to him.)* I do very much hope you'll be at home here. *(The lights fade.)*

Scene 2

11 A.M. on a Tuesday in September. Outside it's pouring rain. Planks of wood are stacked against the wall and the toolbox is out but otherwise there's been no progress. Brandt sits at the table taking notes. Hannah paces excitedly.

BRANDT. "Jesus said."

HANNAH. Already this is enormously complicated.

BRANDT. On the first two words?

HANNAH. Really they should be paying you by the hour.

BRANDT. Lay it on me.

HANNAH. To begin with we should explain that there were somewhere north of thirty gospels written in the years after Jesus' death.

BRANDT. Definitely at least thirty?

HANNAH. Possibly a hundred. Each one of them full of more wise things Jesus might've said and other miracles He might've performed. Including one lovely story where the boy Jesus sculpts several pigeons out of clay and then He waves his arms and they fly away.

BRANDT. And the bishops winnowed all these gospels down because by the end of the second century Christians were being slaughtered wholesale —

HANNAH. — and if the religion was going to survive they couldn't tell so many versions of the story. They chose four gospels because they believed there were four regions of the universe and four winds.

BRANDT. Always nice to see the impeccable logic of the Christian church at work. So then the bishops decide to destroy all the other gospels —

HANNAH. — but some of them were rediscovered at Nag Hammadi. And now there's this one.

BRANDT. And if this was written in 50 or 60 A.D., then it pre-dates all the gospels we already know about —

HANNAH. *(With a quiet fervor.)* — which means it's quite possible this is a rather amazing document. You see, it's a strongly held belief that there was a gospel written much earlier than any of the others that was the source for a great deal of Matthew and Luke.

BRANDT. And you think that's what this might be?

HANNAH. Far too early to tell. But yes, there's a fighting chance that this is the nearest we've ever gotten to the true words of Christ.

BRANDT. And that's why this gospel is so important to you?

HANNAH. *(Brought up short a moment.)* Me personally? You know how I hate these stained-glass windows?

BRANDT. You've made that abundantly clear.

HANNAH. Because as far as I'm concerned they color and shade the true story of Jesus. This is my struggle: I want my windows free of stain, I want a clear view of God. I tried to find it in these gospels but they're tainted with politics too.

BRANDT. So you'd beg to differ with the evangelists who proclaim that the Bible is the inerrant word of God.

HANNAH. The Bible is a self-contradictory, haphazardly edited compilation.

BRANDT. *(Brought up short himself.)* This is going to be a really excellent book.

HANNAH. Two thousand years ago something so extraordinary happened that many of the people who experienced it felt compelled to write it all down. But most of their stories have been lost to us forever. *(Hannah is getting very impassioned. Brandt watches her closely.)* That's why this gospel could be such an enormous gift. In some small way it might cast a pure and necessary light. And then perhaps we can all get ever so much closer to a clear view of God. *(Thomas careens into the room, his clothes and hair completely soaked.)*

THOMAS. It's kind of the end of the world.

HANNAH. I suppose owning an umbrella would be too materialistic for you.

THOMAS. *(Points to the papers on the table.)* Have you found anything in there about a second great flood?

HANNAH. I have it on good authority it'll be fire next time. *(Hannah packs her bag and puts on her scarf.)*

THOMAS. Thought maybe I'd get to work on those bookshelves today.

HANNAH. Signs and wonders everywhere. Get that sweater off before you catch pneumonia.

THOMAS. I'm twenty-six years old.

HANNAH. And I'm only asking that you make it to twenty-seven. I'm off to explain the Nicene Creed to a classroom full of dough-faced Jesus freaks from the Midwest. *(Thomas pulls off his wet sweater. Hannah starts out of the room.)*

BRANDT. I'll see you tomorrow morning at eleven then. Maybe we can get through three or four more words. *(Hannah picks up the first page of the gospel and considers it.)*

HANNAH. This first verse roughly translates as: "Jesus said, I have come to cast fire on the earth and stand guard over it till it blazes." *(On her way out the door.)* Wish me luck in the storm. *(She is gone. Brandt stares after her for a moment and then picks up a few books from the table. Thomas puts on his tool belt and pulls out the planks of wood.)*

THOMAS. I'm probably gonna be making a lot of noise.

BRANDT. Don't worry about me, I'll just be sitting over here trying to teach myself Coptic. A Sisyphean task at best.

THOMAS. Are you her latest disciple?

BRANDT. I'm not sure what that means.

THOMAS. Every term there's another new seminarian all wet behind the ears following her around like a lost orphan. Hate to break it to you but you're a dime a dozen.

BRANDT. Actually I don't go to school here. I'm helping with her book.

THOMAS. *(With a new interest.)* A civilian. We don't see your kind too much around these parts. Still it's amazing how closely you fit the mold.

BRANDT. And what mold is that?

THOMAS. When I was a kid her disciples always looked like my father. Lean, wavy hair, maybe a little wild-eyed. Now they all have a tendency to be roughly my age and general description. I'd be flattered if I wasn't so creeped out.

BRANDT. Rest assured I'm the furthest thing from a seminarian.

THOMAS. But I bet she's already trying to convert you. Don't let her get to you. Forewarned is forearmed. Stay strong. *(Brandt rises. His knapsack slips off his lap and all the contents spill onto the floor. Thomas comes over to help him out.)*

BRANDT. I'm making a huge mess here.

THOMAS. You're in possession of a surprising number of x-rays.

BRANDT. I'm walking around with all these photos of my dad's brain.

THOMAS. Let me take a look at these. *(Thomas lays the x-rays out on the table. They both consider them.)*

BRANDT. The neurosurgeon gave them to me. Of course I have no idea what they mean. Like is this the part of his brain that gave him his strange passion to become a systems analyst? Is that where he stores all his favorite jokes from late-night talk-show hosts? Is this the root of his deep abiding love for pistachio ice cream?

THOMAS. He has a tumor wrapped around the nerves at the base of the stem.

BRANDT. *(Stares at him closely.)* That's impressive and freaky of you.

THOMAS. I went to med school for a while. Till I got fed up with the whole western medical establishment. Granted we're better than anyone else in the world at handling trauma. But we're hopeless in terms of prevention and holistic alternatives. It's arrogant and frankly dangerous and I didn't want any part of it.

BRANDT. They want to do a biopsy. They'll stick a needle up through the roof of his mouth. To find out if it's malignant.

THOMAS. Western medicine in a nutshell. Who cares if it's cancerous? It's a brain tumor. Even if it's benign it'll eventually kill him if they can't nuke it or take it out.

BRANDT. Maybe you should come with me to the neurosurgeon.

THOMAS. No wonder my mother chose you. Almost literally an orphan.

BRANDT. I really don't think Hannah hired me because of my father.

THOMAS. My mother has a tendency to think everything happens for a reason. It kind of comes with the uniform. *(Brandt shifts on his feet, suddenly a little bit uncomfortable.)*

BRANDT. I'm keeping you from your work.

THOMAS. I didn't mean to offend you.

BRANDT. I'm not the least bit offended. *(They both go back to work. After a moment Thomas stops hammering.)*

THOMAS. I don't want to give you the wrong impression. I love my mother more than the world. She was a widow before I was even born, and she cobbled together a truly decent life for me from scraps she found on the side of the road. Which is why it kills me to see her in a job that requires her to systematically lie to everyone.

BRANDT. One thing I already know about your mother, she believes every word she says.

THOMAS. That's the worst part! She's a salesman who's her own best customer. And it's not like she's illiterate trailer trash sending her beauty shop salary to the televangelist. She's fully informed and still she chooses to swallow the Kool-Aid.

BRANDT. She hardly seems like any kind of sheep.

THOMAS. She knows Jesus never claimed to be God, of the four gospels only John even comes close to saying so. Plus Jesus kept saying the apocalypse was coming in his generation, whoops, he was off by nineteen hundred years and counting, so he's hardly omniscient. *(Brandt is a little taken aback. Thomas is on a tear now.)* Then there's the whole fig tree incident: Jesus wants figs but the tree is bare, so he curses it and it dies, but if you're God, for Pete's sake, just make some more figs.

BRANDT. Boy, you sure know your theology, don't you?

THOMAS. *(With a sheepish grin.)* What would you expect, growing up with Hannah? When I was a kid she had me convinced I was the second coming of Christ.

BRANDT. Doesn't every little Christian boy believe that at some point?

THOMAS. Every night before bed she'd read to me from the gospels. Lonely little boy, fiercely protective mother, mysterious absent father, how could I not identify?

BRANDT. Plus now she's got you working as a carpenter.

THOMAS. *(Puts his head in his hands.)* She does! For crying out loud! That didn't even occur to me!

BRANDT. Funny she named you Thomas though. Doubting apostle and all.

THOMAS. Shows how little you know. My parents were studying the gospel of Thomas when they met. He was the minister back then: She was just a religious studies major. See, Thomas believed each person has a direct relationship with God. He was a huge threat to the bishops so John made up the story of doubting Thomas to discredit him.

BRANDT. Looks like she ended up with a doubting Thomas anyway.

THOMAS. Now you start to see how deep the moat is dug. Swim for shore while you've still got the chance. I was nearly a Benedictine monk before I realized how deep Hannah had her hooks in me.

BRANDT. Hold up for a second: You were a Benedictine monk?

THOMAS. Technically no. I'd made a vow of oblation but it takes five years to become a full monk and I quit after nine months. It was kind of great for a while. You get to plant a lot of trees, you learn how to make a number of excellent rice dishes. *(Brandt stares at Thomas, his books and papers forgotten on the table.)* But in the end it was really disappointing. It was all about the bureaucracy of the monastery, whose turn it was to do the laundry and when we should say matins, finally I got fed up and left.

BRANDT. Maybe you should just tell me everything you haven't done, that would save us both a whole lot of time. *(Thomas lifts his shirt up to show Brandt his tool belt.)*

THOMAS. Every time I do something new I carve it on my tool belt. Here's when I had the duck farm. That ended kind of sadly, the ducks would always stick their necks out through the holes in the coop and at night raccoons would come by and rip their heads off.

BRANDT. That does sound a little grisly.

THOMAS. Here's when I taught these Iroquois how to canoe. They wanted to paddle down to the U.N. to protest the loss of their reservation but they didn't know how. Actually I did most of the canoeing myself, they'd walk along the shore until the press showed up, then they'd quickly jump into the canoe and pretend to paddle. Here's when I drove a taxi in St. Paul. Here's when I helped build a yurt.

BRANDT. Now you're just making up words.

THOMAS. I've tried all of these things on for size but none of them seem to fit.

BRANDT. Maybe you're acquiring the skills to invent what you're supposed to do. It'll involve farming, cooking, medicine and sea-worthy vessels. Could be you're gonna create a new utopian society.

THOMAS. Would you follow me around and say encouraging things like that?

BRANDT. Happy to be of service anytime.

THOMAS. I spent my birthday week hiking up the coast of Maine. I thought, if I have any courage at all I really would get lost. Drop myself off in the middle of nowhere without a map, see if I can work out a basic life for myself away from all this nonsense.

BRANDT. You were hiking the coast of Maine?

THOMAS. My grandmother had a house there when I was a kid.

BRANDT. Forgive me for asking, but isn't that where your father died?

THOMAS. I'm surprised Hannah told you about that.

BRANDT. It sounds like it was a terrible accident.

THOMAS. Now I'm a little less surprised.

BRANDT. I hope I'm not being insensitive.

THOMAS. It's not like she flat-out lied. It's just the circumstances of my father's death are notoriously slippery to the grasp. *(Brandt stares at Thomas closely. Thomas picks at his fingernail.)* They were up at my grandmother's house. It was their last holiday for a while: Mmy mom was a few months pregnant with me. They were lying on the jetty. My dad kissed my mom's belly and she closed her eyes and he walked into the ocean. When she opened her eyes again he was too far out for her to reach. *(Thomas speaks evenly and simply. Outside the rain pours down.)* To this day she doesn't know if he meant to do it. The waves were choppy all of a sudden, he wasn't a strong enough swimmer to be in so deep, he'd been moody lately but his moods had always lifted before. It's just one of those cases where the facts don't help.

BRANDT. I didn't know any of that.

THOMAS. Now you see why you have to watch out for my mother. She only tells the part of a story she can handle. *(They consider each other a moment. Thomas reaches over a pile of books and pulls out a large box.)* This is his collection of balsa wood model airplanes. With hand-painted insignias of all the great nations of Europe. My father was far-ranging but fickle in his enthusiasms. Sound familiar?

BRANDT. I wasn't going to say anything.

THOMAS. These I haven't had the courage to crack yet. *(Thomas pulls out a stack of books. Brandt looks through them.)*

BRANDT. All of these were his Bibles?

THOMAS. Oxford, New King James, Greek, Latin. My father was nothing if not a completist. All dog-eared with underlinings and highlightings and notes scribbled in the margins everywhere. *(Thomas picks up one of the Bibles and starts leafing through it.)*

BRANDT. So what made you suddenly decide to look through all his stuff?

THOMAS. *(Shrugs his shoulders.)* I just turned twenty-six. Now I'm older than my father ever was.

BRANDT. Is there anything in particular you're expecting to find?

THOMAS. *(With a sly smile.)* I suspect I'm just rummaging through a lot of worthless old junk hoping against hope that some long-dead man will have a few words of wisdom for me. I am my mother's son after all.

BRANDT. Does Hannah know this is why you came home?

THOMAS. We kind of don't tell each other everything. *(Hungrily Thomas leans in and kisses Brandt on the mouth. Instinctively Brandt recoils, pulling away.)*

BRANDT. Boy, you really know how to freak a guy out, don't you?

THOMAS. Did I just make a huge mistake?

BRANDT. It's just a terrible idea for so many reasons.

THOMAS. I thought maybe you were looking my way.

BRANDT. *(Looks down at the floor.)* You've got a big scar on your elbow, I noticed that the first day I met you. There's a strawberry birthmark at the back of your neck, it flushes red when you get excited. Also a bruise on your forearm which you acquired sometime between Tuesday and Friday.

THOMAS. Then I have to say I'm more than a little perplexed.

BRANDT. For one thing I don't think Hannah would be all that enthusiastic about this.

THOMAS. You don't know the half of it. She was far and away the happiest with me when I was a monk.

BRANDT. And I did come into this house as her employee.

THOMAS. I won't tell her if you won't.

BRANDT. *(Hesitates a moment, then:)* See, when I'm not here I'm at one hospital or another. So things are pretty raw for me at the moment. I'm just being held together by straight pins.

THOMAS. Or maybe we could help each other out for a little while.

BRANDT. *(Gently but firmly.)* That's exactly why this can't go any further: because right now I really don't need anyone who'll only be around for a little while.

THOMAS. Too bad the weather isn't fairer. *(It's still very charged between them. Brandt grabs his coat from the rack and heads toward the door.)*

BRANDT. I should really get going. I've got lunch with my parents.

THOMAS. Don't let me keep you from anything.

BRANDT. I'm really glad you looked my way though.

THOMAS. Anytime. *(Brandt is gone. Thomas stares after him for a moment. Then he picks up one of the Bibles and starts leafing through it. Outside the rain falls harder and harder. The lights fade.)*

Scene 3

Very late at night on a Friday in October. The lamps bathe the room in a warm orange glow. Outside the windows it's pitch black. On the table is the detritus of a Thai takeout dinner and a half-empty bottle of wine. Essentially no progress on the bookshelves. Brandt and Hannah sit together at the table, pulling an all-nighter.

BRANDT. *(Reading from his notes.)* "Jesus said, my yoke is good to bear, my burden is light."

HANNAH. Now this verse appears almost identically in Matthew and Luke, and in the gnostic gospel of Thomas. Which suggests it's authentic to Jesus. It also sounds like Him: He often spoke in paradoxes.

BRANDT. So does that make it more likely that this was the first gospel?

HANNAH. I'm afraid my jury is still very much out on that. What I can say with authority is that I'm getting a very sharp picture of the author of this particular gospel.

BRANDT. And is this conclusion based on scholarship or theology?

HANNAH. First off it's clear he's well-educated. Maybe even a little over-educated. In my eyes he's a fairly young man adrift in the big city. Now that I think about it he's more than a little like you.

BRANDT. *(Hesitates a moment, then.)* Do you ever wonder if you're just making all of this up?

HANNAH. I'm not sure I understand what you mean.

BRANDT. All this studying, comparing one gospel to another, factoring in all these lost and discredited texts — do you ever worry you're just creating the Jesus you'd personally like to believe in?

HANNAH. I work very rigorously to guard against that.

BRANDT. But I've only been working with you two months and already I can see how jerry-built the whole apparatus is. Mark ends with an empty tomb and no hint of resurrection. Matthew is frantic to quash the rumors the disciples didn't just steal Jesus' body.

HANNAH. My goodness, I've taught you well, haven't I?

BRANDT. Take all that away and what you're left with are the pleasant sayings of a reasonably charismatic teacher. There were so many crucifixions in those years, the countryside around Jerusalem was deforested. What makes this one so special?

HANNAH. Do you really think you're the first person to make this argument?

BRANDT. How can you look at all this so closely without losing your faith?

HANNAH. This is not a question for the book.

BRANDT. If you can answer it, I can write the book much more effectively.

HANNAH. As you say, I've studied all this a great deal. I'm well-traveled and well read and I've heard most of the stories people tell to make sense of the world and this is the one that speaks to me. *(The lamplight silhouettes Hannah against the pitch-black sky. Brandt sits still in his chair.)* The idea that a helpless infant in a stable is actually the most powerful creature in the universe. And the death of a man in agony on a cross is not a defeat but the greatest victory in the history of the world. That there is always the possibility of redemption. That we can make each other whole. To me that's truer than anything you can prove. This is what faith means: You climb all the steps you can and then you take a leap.

BRANDT. Sometimes I get the impression that you're trying to save my soul.

HANNAH. *(Considers him very closely.)* I want to be especially careful in our discussion of this verse.

BRANDT. What exactly are you concerned about?

HANNAH. This is one of the few verses to deal with the problem of pain.

BRANDT. Pain?

HANNAH. Specifically the question of why God would choose to create a world that's so filled with suffering.

BRANDT. The yoke and the burden.

HANNAH. I'm worried this might be a little tender for you at the moment.

BRANDT. Actually I'm dying to hear what Christ has to say on the topic. *(It's very intense between them. Hannah hesitates for a moment.)*

HANNAH. It's the Church's position that a great deal of suffering is a direct result of our turning away from God.

BRANDT. Therefore if we all behaved properly, that pain could be avoided.

HANNAH. Exactly. But a good and decent man who's having

poison injected into his veins in the hopes that this will shrink the tumor growing in his brain — why would God allow such a thing?

BRANDT. The official line is that ever since the fall of Adam we're all condemned to suffer sickness and death. Isn't that right?

HANNAH. What a barbarous piece of theology. To believe we're responsible for the sins of our most distant ancestors.

BRANDT. So I take it you have a different explanation.

HANNAH. *(As delicately as possible.)* As I see it, the only logical way to explain why God permits pain to exist is that for some reason it's necessary. He's only interested in our bodies because they house our souls. And perhaps our souls are only forged in pain and burnished in death.

BRANDT. *(Stares at her in disbelief.)* Of course you realize that's offensively uncomforting.

HANNAH. I know it's a terribly hard road that God makes us travel. But if we submit to the pain, if we let His will be done, then we might find that His yoke is good to bear, His burden is light.

BRANDT. But isn't that even worse? How can you have faith in a God who created the world just to torture everyone in it? *(Thomas sidles through the door and leans against the wall lazily.)*

THOMAS. My mother is getting you drunk.

HANNAH. Nothing wrong with a glass or two on a Friday night.

THOMAS. Actually Hannah knows this excellent magic trick. She waves her hand over the bottle and suddenly it's the blood of Christ.

HANNAH. Just plain old wine here. *(Thomas heads over to the table, a little unsteady on his feet. He's a friendly and amiable drunk.)*

BRANDT. Looks like you've been tipping a few back yourself.

THOMAS. I'm an unspecified number of sheets to the wind.

BRANDT. You're sort of listing a little to the right.

THOMAS. Quite the party here, kicking off the weekend with a little Pinot and pad thai and the Nag Hammadi scrolls.

HANNAH. I'm not even going to ask where you've been.

THOMAS. There are any number of watering holes in this city full of any number of friendly souls in search of fellow-feeling. *(Thomas sits down at the table and reaches out for the wine bottle.)*

HANNAH. Aren't you maybe over your limit for the night?

THOMAS. One more will tuck me happily into bed. Jesus would certainly approve. He was quite the hedonist Himself, wasn't He? Partied till dawn at that wedding in Cana. *(Thomas refills their glasses and swigs from the bottle.)*

HANNAH. No question about it. Of course He knew how to

hold His liquor. And I doubt He ever went to a singles bar.

THOMAS. Nobody's called them singles bars for twenty-five years.

HANNAH. One thing He made perfectly clear is that once you sleep with someone you're married in the eyes of God.

THOMAS. Regrettably in God's eyes I'm a bigamist. Or at least a Mormon. Are you worried there's a huge punishment in store for me?

HANNAH. It's less about punishments and more about consequences. I'd like you alive in the world for as long as possible. *(Hannah holds Thomas in her gaze. Thomas smiles slightly.)*

THOMAS. Of course if God is all-powerful and all-knowing then He's already determined whether or not I'm destined for the scrap heap.

HANNAH. I refuse to discuss predestination and free will with you again.

THOMAS. Either He controls everything or He doesn't. And if He does then I don't see how I have any choice in the matter of my behavior.

HANNAH. My son's favorite pastime is backing me into a corner.

THOMAS. If I'm going down anyway I might as well make it count.

HANNAH. What you fail to understand is that God doesn't live in time like we do. He looks at your life like it's the view out this window and each light in every building is one moment. He sees it all at once but it's always in your power whether to light the lamps.

THOMAS. If God wants me to be different, I don't know why He didn't make me that way. Would've saved everybody a whole lot of trouble.

HANNAH. Yes, well, it's rather like being a parent, isn't it? You give your child all the freedom in the world, knowing full well he may use that freedom to turn away from you. *(Thomas stares at Hannah carefully. Hannah smiles placidly at him.)*

THOMAS. But I don't believe Jesus forbids widows from remarrying, does He?

HANNAH. In fact He heartily encourages it.

THOMAS. Because there are also consequences to sitting at home alone every night. Not the least of which is that your life goes by.

HANNAH. I'm not alone in case you hadn't noticed. *(Thomas looks at Brandt and Hannah and a grin grows on his face.)*

THOMAS. Alone together.

HANNAH. I'm not keeping you from anybody, am I, Brandt?

BRANDT. *(With a mordant laugh.)* Nobody's waiting up for me, don't worry about that.

THOMAS. *(Turns to Hannah intensely.)* It kills me how much you hoard yourself away. Do you ever think maybe Jesus doesn't want all this attention, that some of the love you're giving Him might be better spent elsewhere?

HANNAH. I think there's a lot to be said for the life I've chosen. I'm trying to love everyone equally, without any possessiveness.

THOMAS. Speaking as your son, I have to say, if you're trying to love without possessiveness, you've got a hell of a long way to go.

HANNAH. *(With a surge of emotion.)* Well, why shouldn't I be frightened for you? You're so wasteful with yourself. You wander down every stray path in the road, you give yourself away so easily to any stranger who passes by.

THOMAS. Who or what I give myself away to is none of your concern —

HANNAH. Forgive me for trying so desperately to pull you back from the precipice. Because pardon me if I'm terrified that one day soon you'll give yourself away for good.

THOMAS. Hey, if it makes you this miserable to have me around, I can be gone by morning. I'm an expert at traveling light. *(Hannah's whole body tenses up. Brandt shifts in his chair. Thomas swigs from the bottle of wine.)*

HANNAH. I think it's past your bedtime.

THOMAS. You guys hear about the meteor shower coming next month?

BRANDT. Think we'll be able to see it in the city? *(Dreamily Thomas sinks into a chair and leans it back against the wall.)*

THOMAS. Always makes me sad, though — poor things, tumbling through space, all they want is someplace safe to land. They throw themselves toward us but we just burn them to bits. *(Thomas leans back and closes his eyes. Hannah watches him closely.)*

BRANDT. I was a kid the last time Halley's Comet came around. I made my dad take me to the woods in Jersey on a school night so I could see it pass over. All we saw were a bunch of planes and this teenage couple making out in the bushes. Fun night though anyway. *(Thomas is leaning back, his eyes closed, his mouth lolling open.)*

HANNAH. I'm afraid he's fast asleep.

BRANDT. He can fall asleep sitting up?

HANNAH. He can fall asleep in the middle of a three-ring circus. *(Nudging Thomas gently.)* Hey, my love, hey.

29

THOMAS. *(His eyes slowly opening.)* Did I drift off?

HANNAH. All the way to dreamland.

THOMAS. *(Rising to his feet.)* Guess I'd better trundle off to bed.

HANNAH. Make sure you get all the way to your room, all right? Don't stop and curl up in the hall. *(Rubbing his eyes, Thomas lumbers toward the door. On his way out he tousles Brandt's hair very lightly.)*

THOMAS. Take care of my mother for me. *(Thomas heads off to bed. Brandt and Hannah watch after him.)*

BRANDT. We should probably start cleaning up. *(Brandt starts to organize his notebooks. Hannah sits silently for a moment before she speaks.)*

HANNAH. How much time have you been spending with my son?

BRANDT. Our shifts here in the library sometimes overlap.

HANNAH. May I ask, how does he seem to you?

BRANDT. *(A little uncomfortable.)* Hmm. Well. He's really enthusiastic, that's for sure. Even if his enthusiasms change from day to day, or minute to minute. I know he feels very strongly about holistic medicine and the wetlands and socialism and certain brands of peanut butter.

HANNAH. I'm sure he has a lot to say about me.

BRANDT. From what I've seen, he doesn't say anything behind your back that he wouldn't happily say to your face.

HANNAH. You know he and I don't see very much of each other.

BRANDT. I think he did mention something about that.

HANNAH. He started running away from home when he was ten and it's a habit he's never been able to break. Whole years go by, I only know where he is from the hitchhiking tickets I get in the mail. *(Brandt is standing now, clutching his notebooks in his hands.)* I'm not even quite certain how he manages to earn a living. He does odd jobs here and there, I guess, plus he's got a trust from his grandmother, just enough rope to hang himself.

BRANDT. It's good you can provide him with a safe place to come home to.

HANNAH. The main reason he's come home is to look through his father's things. He actually thinks I don't know that. *(It's quiet. Briefly Hannah sorts through some papers on the table.)* If it's not too personal, do your parents know you're homosexual?

BRANDT. *(With a laugh.)* Actually I think they figured it out long before I did.

HANNAH. I hope they've been decent about it.

BRANDT. One day when I was eleven I had this overpowering urge to hug my friend Kevin on the playground. I came home and told my father about it, and he said it was only natural for a kid my age to be in love with everybody. It was kind of the perfect thing to say.

HANNAH. And have you ever brought a young man home to meet them?

BRANDT. *(Shaking his head.)* I'm afraid there hasn't been anyone who's stuck around long enough for them to meet.

HANNAH. Is that a veiled way of saying you're promiscuous?

BRANDT. *(A slight attack of coughing.)* I certainly didn't expect to have this conversation tonight.

HANNAH. If you're at all uncomfortable we can stop.

BRANDT. It's just your collar is a little intimidating.

HANNAH. I'm not trying to be your confessor. Wrong denomination anyway. I'm asking because I hope I've become something of a friend.

BRANDT. *(Considers a moment, then:)* All right. Sure. I had a few years when I was a little free with myself. See, I've always been very shy. And I used to cultivate these impossible unspoken crushes that could never go anywhere. After a while I just got so sick to death of yearning and pining.

HANNAH. Believe me, I know the feeling.

BRANDT. So it was nice for a time to give myself away to lots of different strangers, to pretend it didn't matter. But I had to stop because in the end it really does matter, doesn't it, more than anything.

HANNAH. But so far you haven't found anyone for yourself?

BRANDT. It just hasn't come around for me in a very long while.

HANNAH. Not for me either.

BRANDT. It's an excellent life though. I make my own hours. Awake by the late single digits, five hours of work, then grill myself lunch on the George Foreman. Teach an English class at NYU to put cash in my pocket and make sure I'm out in the world. Dinner with friends then drift off happily to sleep with the late-night TV. *(A small smile.)* If it keeps on like this much longer it'll be unbearable.

HANNAH. I know it's been a little strange in my house. So I feel it's important that I explain some things.

BRANDT. I don't want to get in the middle of anything.

HANNAH. Unfortunately you got tied up in it just walking through the door. I'm only trying to prevent any unnecessary entanglements. *(Hannah stares out at the pitch-black night. Brandt is still.)* Thomas was sixteen the first time he really ran away from home. He

31

took his life-guarding money and bought a bus ticket to Arizona. He vanished for five months. The detectives I hired finally found him in the desert just outside Phoenix, in a little hut he'd built for himself. By then he only weighed eighty-six pounds.

BRANDT. Teenage boys do stupid things.

HANNAH. Yes, of course, but when he spends his birthday hiking the coast of Maine just so he can see the place where his father drowned, wouldn't it be remiss of me not to be frightened for him? *(She turns to face him. He shifts uneasily on the balls of his feet.)*

BRANDT. I'm not sure exactly what you want from me.

HANNAH. First of all, I trust that you're not playing with him.

BRANDT. What on earth do you mean by that?

HANNAH. He arranges to be home when he knows you're around. And the only time he even pretends to work on these bookshelves is when you're here doing research on your own. I'm not completely obtuse.

BRANDT. Do you honestly think that I'm capable of leading Thomas astray?

HANNAH. *(Gently but firmly.)* You've caught him at an especially tender moment. And it would be awfully irresponsible for you to take advantage of him because you don't have anything else on your plate right now.

BRANDT. With all due respect you're really out of line here. For one thing I don't think Thomas is in any danger. He's frustrated, sure, and he's digging through his history to figure out how to move forward. I think that's a really admirable thing to do. *(Brandt is surprised at the extent of his own feeling. Hannah watches him, her expression unreadable.)* And given your history I understand why all of this scares you, but in my opinion you're reading the cards all wrong.

HANNAH. You don't know how lovely it would be if that were true.

BRANDT. And I'm certainly not playing with him. Thomas just about kills me. I can't say his name without it catching in my throat, fifty times a day I stop in the middle of the street to wonder what he's doing, if I had any courage at all I'd fall in love with him. *(Hannah stares at him for a moment. When she speaks again, her voice is quiet and achingly vulnerable.)*

HANNAH. Then why don't you?

BRANDT. *(At a loss for a moment.)* First of all I thought this was something you don't want.

HANNAH. I don't want you tumbling into anything with your eyes closed. But if you need my permission you have it wholeheartedly.

BRANDT. I'm not quite sure I understand what you're asking.

HANNAH. I'm not asking you to counterfeit any feelings you don't have. I certainly don't want you to do anything on my behalf. But if you think you can love him then please just don't stop yourself.

BRANDT. To put it mildly this is a very strange request.

HANNAH. I'm sort of at the end of my tether. I try to help him but everything I do just muddies the water even worse.

BRANDT. But what could I possibly do for him?

HANNAH. If he's found someone who feels like home to him, maybe that would help him through this especially delicate year. And then maybe he'll be out of the woods for good.

BRANDT. That's a pretty enormous responsibility you're giving me.

HANNAH. I think you could help keep him safe just by standing next to him.

BRANDT. I have to admit I'm more than a little hesitant to take this on.

HANNAH. Because of your father?

BRANDT. At least partly.

HANNAH. But isn't this exactly what he wants for you? Wouldn't he be overjoyed that you've found someone?

BRANDT. Of course he would.

HANNAH. Then forgive me but I genuinely don't see the problem here.

BRANDT. I'm sure you've noticed your son has a tendency not to stay in one place very long. If I couldn't keep him it would break my heart.

HANNAH. But it's the worst thing, isn't it, not to love someone when you can.

BRANDT. I'm afraid I won't be any use to him.

HANNAH. You asked me how I keep my faith in the face of all the evidence to the contrary. But if you take God away, the world is no less horrible. Without God the world is only pain with no chance of redemption. And I can't believe that when I look at you. *(Brandt looks up at her. She speaks with nothing but tender compassion.)* Because here you are in awful pain for your father but your heart is still full to bursting: In the depths of your soul you reach out for someone you love. What is that if not a blessing? *(Hannah moves to Brandt in the lamp light. Outside and all around them there is nothing but darkness.)* Here's where I see God: He's your aching heart in the dead of winter. He's reaching out to you right now with all the power to ease your pain and lift your burden. Will you take His hand?

ACT TWO

Scene 1

Dusk on a Sunday in November. The sunset casts an orange-purple glow across the room. A telescope has been set up in front of the window. Brandt and Thomas are kissing.

THOMAS. Watch the skies.

BRANDT. I thought we were going up on the roof.

THOMAS. Officially it's a fire hazard to sit on the roof of this building. Although I fully intend to sneak up there once the day-shift security guards go home. This is just a stop-gap solution. *(Thomas finishes assembling the telescope. Brandt hovers nearby.)*

BRANDT. I'm an excellent astronomer myself. Look, you can already see the North Star, and there's Alpha Centauri, closest star except the sun, and there's Orion's Belt, see? Actually I don't know what any of these stars are, I'm just making this up to impress you.

THOMAS. Hate to break it to you but I already figured that out.

BRANDT. There's the big salad tongs and the little salad tongs, and right up there, that's the dental star.

THOMAS. I was an astronomy major for about five minutes at my third or fourth college. Lately I'm thinking I should take it up again. Go out to Maria Mitchell Observatory, see if they'll let me sweep the floors in exchange for some night classes.

BRANDT. Is there really any call for an itinerant astronomer these days?

THOMAS. I don't see why not. I'll travel from town to town, pointing out various planets and constellations to the villagers, and they'll invite me into their homes for cornbread and mulled cider. It sounds like an excellent plan. This room is kind of a disaster. *(Brandt unfolds the picnic blanket.)*

BRANDT. Somebody should really be building shelves for all these books. *(Thomas picks up one of the Bibles and pages through it.)*

THOMAS. Look what I found pressed between the pages of the

Revised Standard New King James edition: beech leaves every-where for some reason. *(Thomas extracts a dried-up old leaf from between the pages.)*

BRANDT. You're not actually going to read through all of his Bibles.

THOMAS. Just the sections he marked up. From what I've gathered he was especially interested in Paul's concepts of faith and love but he didn't pay much attention to genealogy and dietary restrictions.

BRANDT. I can't understand why you won't talk to Hannah about all this.

THOMAS. In case you haven't noticed it's a little difficult to extract information from her on this particular topic.

BRANDT. Why don't you just start by asking about the beech leaves and see how far that takes you?

THOMAS. Have you ever looked through any of your dad's stuff from when he was your age?

BRANDT. A few years ago I found his college entrance essay in the attic. Turns out he wanted to be a writer when he started at UVA. but his folks made him major in business. He never men-tioned that to me when I was growing up, he certainly never set me on this path, but it did make me wonder how much of my life is just his unlived. *(Thomas pages through the Bible.)* My dad was so impressed when you yelled at his nurse today.

THOMAS. I clocked it: She took twenty minutes to respond to his page. He was sitting there with that empty I.V. stuck in his arm. Sunday staff is the worst. Nothing but greenhorns and malcontents.

BRANDT. Believe it or not he's actually in much better shape than he was. I mean besides the vomiting and that weird moment when he felt like he'd snorted hot wasabi up his nose.

THOMAS. Fifty years from now we'll look back on radiation and it'll seem like some barbaric torture, like leeches.

BRANDT. My folks were over the moon to meet you.

THOMAS. To be honest I was totally freaked out about it. I was pet-rified I'd walk in the door and they'd stare at us with daggers in their eyes, imagining us in various baroque upsetting sexual positions.

BRANDT. Are you kidding? My parents have been waiting so long for this day. They always said all they wanted is for me to find someone who makes me happy. I think today they were incredibly relieved to discover that really is all they want for me.

THOMAS. I loved all your mom's photos: Brandt from infancy to adulthood always with that secret little half-smile, your eyes focused just to the left of the lens looking off in the distance at something.

BRANDT. I'm pretty sure I was looking for you.

THOMAS. I was thinking today I should go to nursing school. I'd like to do hospice work, somewhere in the desert, New Mexico maybe, help people live gracefully at the end. What do you think of that?

BRANDT. I think you've got no shortage of escape plans, my friend. *(Thomas leans in and kisses Brandt.)*

THOMAS. This is going so much better than the first time we tried this.

BRANDT. You know, when I was a kid I thought kissing was just something grown-ups did to signify to the world that they were in love. When somebody finally kissed me, I was so shocked there was actually a physical sensation attached to the gesture I burst into tears.

THOMAS. In junior high this girl Caitlin took me under her wing. She'd practice with me behind the 7-11. She taught me how to loosen up my tongue, she told me to keep my hands in my pockets because that drives the ladies crazy. Now anybody compliments me on my kissing, I think, that's Caitlin.

BRANDT. What a heartbreaker you must've been back then.

THOMAS. Man, I was desperate to be a rebel. I was a Punk and a New Waver and a Straight Edger and I had all these asymmetrical haircuts. Of course, once I figured out that I actually wanted to kiss boys, I really took off full steam ahead in the rebellion department.

BRANDT. You know what I thought about, watching my dad today? I had these awful nightmares when I was little. Made me scared to go to bed. My dad would lie down next to me till I fell asleep. *(Thomas holds Brandt and lightly strokes his arm with his fingers.)* One morning I woke up and he was still asleep next to me. It was like I'd gotten away with something amazing. Let's face it, in the most natural way he was definitely the first man I ever loved.

THOMAS. I found a scrapbook my dad made of a cross-country trip he took. One summer he got it in his head to be a traveling missionary. He'd just drive around and stop off anytime people needed help building their houses or fixing their cars or whatever. I was thinking it might be amazing to retrace his steps all these years later, see how much the country's changed, you know?

BRANDT. *(With a slight smile.)* So when are you planning to leave? *(Hannah comes in from downstairs. She smiles to see them. The boys pull away slightly, a bit sheepish.)*

HANNAH. Don't let an old lady interrupt.

BRANDT. You're not interrupting anything.

HANNAH. Disaster at vespers. We have new altar candles, five feet high, so they come right up to the noses of the acolytes. Whole service they're breathing in toxic fumes. The first boy fainted during the homily. By the offertory they were dropping like flies.

BRANDT. You had to call off Holy Eucharist on account of injuries?

HANNAH. It's probably a first in the annals of the Episcopal church.

THOMAS. Speaking of which, things are about to start falling from the sky. *(Hannah hangs up her jacket and scarf and turns to Brandt.)*

HANNAH. I looked at your first three chapters this afternoon. I must say you're doing a sterling job at giving order to my digressions.

BRANDT. Honestly I'm just trying not to trip over my own feet. *(Hannah picks up the manuscript from the table and leafs through it.)*

HANNAH. And I must say I'm falling more and more in love with the Jesus of this gospel. When He says you must love your brother as your soul, you must guard him like the inside of your eye, and then the kingdom of heaven will be spread out upon the earth: I have to admit I'm seeing evidence of that everywhere. It's just such a wonderful mystery to be living inside. *(This last is said with a pointed nod to Brandt and Thomas. Brandt toes the floor with his shoe.)*

THOMAS. So long as we're living in mysteries, do you have any idea why there are all these beech leaves in the pages of this Bible? *(Thomas hands the Bible to Hannah. Brandt watches them both closely. The air in the room is very still.)*

HANNAH. Is there anything in particular you're looking for here?

THOMAS. I'll figure out what I'm looking for once I find it.

HANNAH. *(Shifts her gaze to Brandt.)* Is there some way you could use your influence over my son to gently persuade him to give up this scavenger hunt?

BRANDT. You know better than anybody how stubborn he is.

HANNAH. *(Turns back to Thomas.)* Yes, well, I wonder how far you plan to take this. Are you going to read through all his old term papers and report cards?

THOMAS. Maybe if you'd be a little more forthcoming with information I wouldn't be forced to dig so deep into the archives.

HANNAH. What is it exactly that you'd like me to tell you?

THOMAS. At the moment I'm just asking why all the beech leaves.

HANNAH. *(Takes a deep breath, then.)* Those last few months, all of a sudden he was obsessed with the beeches in your grandmother's backyard. We'd sit in the grass and look up at the moon through the branches and he'd collect all these leaves and press them between the pages of his Bible.

THOMAS. *(Gestures to the Bible.)* And do you have any thoughts on why he was so obsessed with Paul's letters to the Corinthians?

HANNAH. Actually I think I'm the one who did all this highlighting.

THOMAS. *(A groan of dismay.)* You mean I've been reading your notes all this time?

BRANDT. *(With a sheepish laugh.)* This is why we should always be sure to authenticate our sources.

HANNAH. What good is all this going to do you?

THOMAS. I'm just curious why the beech leaves and the model planes and the Raymond Chandler paperbacks and the fifty different recordings of the Beethoven piano concertos.

HANNAH. All his fleeting obsessions. He'd pray and fast for days, then he'd eat a steak and sleep for a week. He'd come home from his missions and stare at the walls. Back then it seemed like fervor but of course nowadays they have pills for that sort of thing.

THOMAS. So nobody knew how far gone he was?

HANNAH. I traveled this road long before you and it leads nowhere.

THOMAS. And you honestly never wonder why anymore?

HANNAH. *(Extends her arms helplessly.)* He got too angry or too sad or maybe too tired. Or else suddenly he found himself in too deep. Lately I think it was something in between: Without knowing quite why he put himself in a position where any shift in the tides would just carry him away.

THOMAS. Of course one explanation is he didn't want to have a child.

HANNAH. Yes, well, if you lived your whole life and that thought never crossed your mind, it would've been such a wonderful thing.

THOMAS. And you're really not angry that he left you all alone?

HANNAH. The truth is whatever pain I feel helps me with my work. Because what happened to me is in no way special: Everyone we love on earth we lose. So in the end maybe all we're doing here is teaching each other how God loves us.

THOMAS. But isn't that a really lonely way to live your life?

HANNAH. Except I think loneliness is an enormous blessing. It reminds us that there's something beyond this life. After all, if there's a longing inside us that nothing in this world can satisfy, doesn't it follow that we weren't made for this world?

THOMAS. That's the most ridiculous thing I've ever heard.

HANNAH. This is why you can never be still, my son. Because you believe your loneliness is somehow wrong, that it can be cured by a new view out the window or a different face over the breakfast juice.

THOMAS. It makes you crazy when I'm here and it makes you crazy when I'm gone. I wonder what exactly you'd like me to do with my life.

HANNAH. There's a room down the hall, a few months ago it was just a bed and a desk and four bare walls. Every morning I walk past and I see something new there: tennis shoes from the Salvation Army, a stack of books from the Strand, a pile of rocks for some reason. *(Hannah goes to Thomas and tousles his hair very tentatively.)* More and more it belongs to you again and the only thing I wish is for you to live there as long as you want. I just want this to be your home whenever you need it to be, that's all.

THOMAS. Let's just see how the days keep coming, is that all right?

HANNAH. I think I'll leave you boys in peace.

BRANDT. Please let us know if we're keeping you awake.

HANNAH. Lately I drift off to the murmur of your voices down the hall. They're my favorite sounds to fall asleep to.

BRANDT. Are you sure you don't want to stay up with us?

HANNAH. I have to rest my tired eyes. I'll see you both in the morning. I hope the sky puts on a wonderful show for you. *(Hannah goes out to the bedroom. Brandt stares after her. Thomas throws up his hands, exasperated.)*

THOMAS. Alone at last.

BRANDT. I think she wanted to stay with us.

THOMAS. You shouldn't encourage her or else she'll never leave us alone.

BRANDT. At least she cleared up the mystery of why all the beech leaves. *(Thomas starts packing the stack of Bibles back into their boxes.)*

THOMAS. I can't believe I spent the last four months reading twenty different translations of Leviticus and in the end it was all her notes. It would be great if I could locate at least one centimeter of my life that she's not completely wrapped up in.

BRANDT. I think maybe you're a little too hard on her sometimes.

THOMAS. Yeah, well, she has this tendency to look at me like I'm in too deep and she's standing helpless on some distant shore. I know it's only out of love but it's impossible to live with.

BRANDT. Except I really don't know how you're ever going to get anywhere with her when you always cut and run at the first sign of smoke.

THOMAS. I never said that I was going to cut and run.

BRANDT. It's just kind of obvious the thought has been crossing your mind. (*Thomas shifts his feet a bit and extends his arms to the boxes.*)

THOMAS. I'm certainly not leaving with all this stuff to sort through.

BRANDT. And do you have any plans after that?

THOMAS. In case you hadn't noticed I live kind of a planless life.

BRANDT. I know we've been dealing with this only on a day-to-day basis.

THOMAS. In my opinion that's the best way to deal with everything.

BRANDT. But your mind starts building things on its own. In my head I'm sitting at a desk somewhere and you're coming up the steps, home from the hospice or the observatory or wherever. I just wonder if you're building anything like that yourself.

THOMAS. (*Smiling slightly.*) Any chance you'd like to come with me?

BRANDT. (*With a laugh.*) Is that a serious invitation?

THOMAS. Couldn't hurt you to see the country. Give you lots of fun facts for your arsenal. Plus your kind of work you can do anywhere.

BRANDT. I should point out that at the moment I'm kind of broke.

THOMAS. You're looking at an expert on living hand-to-mouth.

BRANDT. (*As delicately as possible.*) But you know I've got to stay close by right now. I'm somebody's only son. So it's my job to watch him when he gets sick, it's my job to bury him. That's part of the deal, isn't it?

THOMAS. I guess you're a way better son than I am.

BRANDT. It's another reason why I wish you wouldn't leave. Because I look at the two of you and you're twisted into knots but at bottom there's love, and neither one of you is dead yet, so I think you've got to try and get through, if that's really what you want.

THOMAS. These days I think it's the only thing I want in the world. (*They are very close to each other. Brandt lets a smile cross his face.*)

BRANDT. So what do you say we head up to the roof? (*Thomas picks up the Bible again and starts leafing through the pages.)*

THOMAS. *(Reads from the Bible.)* When I was a child I spoke as a child, I understood as a child, but when I became a man, I put away childish things. *(Brandt tackles Thomas and tries to pull the Bible out of his hands.)*

BRANDT. Mercy! Please! I'm begging you! No more scripture!

THOMAS. My opportunities for unfettered research are few and far between.

BRANDT. You don't know how much I'd like to have one hour when I'm not grappling with the question of original sin. *(Brandt gives up the fight and sprawls out on the picnic blanket.)*

THOMAS. You're the soul of patience, do you know that?

BRANDT. To be honest there's a more selfish reason I'm trying to keep you from your work. Because now I know that once you finish you might leave town. And I'm not terribly holy when I'm faced with the prospect of losing something I love. *(A grin slowly forms on Thomas's face. He picks up the Bible.)*

THOMAS. I've got something for you. *(Thomas fans open the Bible over Brandt's head. Leaves fall out from between the pages and cascade all over Brandt and the picnic blanket. Thomas leans over Brandt and kisses him amid the leaves.)*

BRANDT. I suddenly have the feeling nobody's watching the skies tonight. *(The lights fade.)*

Scene 2

A Wednesday morning in December. White-grey light from the overcast sky pokes in through the windows. Brandt and Hannah work at the table. Thomas is unpacking the box of his father's model airplanes.

BRANDT. — and in the afterword you're finally going to have to take a stand on whether or not you believe this is the authentic Jesus.

HANNAH. But I'm afraid there's no way I can say that.

BRANDT. Then I don't understand: How can we draw any definite conclusions here if you know you'll never even get close to an answer?

41

HANNAH. Even if I do decide this was the source for Matthew and Luke … it was still written at least twenty years after Jesus died. Decades of the story passing on the wind, getting tangled and twisted every inch of the way.

THOMAS. If it's all right I'm going to keep these planes in my room. I want to tack them all up to the ceiling and make a giant mobile.

HANNAH. Do whatever you'd like: It's your home as much as mine.

BRANDT. But just so I can have something to hold onto, can you at least give me your best guess from all this evidence?

HANNAH. *(Considers for a moment.)* I think He was lonelier than any of us. He was in the world, and the world was made by Him, but the world didn't know Him. He came to live among the children He loved so dearly, but all we did was ridicule Him and turn away from Him and eventually murder Him. *(As Brandt listens to her, tears form in the corners of his eyes.)* But He gave us this enormous gift. In His brief time here, He showed us how to live a perfect life: how to love each other, how to submit to joy and pain, and how to die. *(Brandt puts his head down and starts to cry quietly. Hannah and Thomas look up at him in concern.)* I'm sorry: Have I upset you?

BRANDT. It's an impossible day is all.

THOMAS. Did something happen with your dad?

BRANDT. *(Waves it away with his hand.)* Nothing really. It's just, this morning it became crystal clear that all the treatments have been worse than pointless. So now the only thing that's left to talk about is his quality of life.

HANNAH. But why on earth did you come to work?

BRANDT. This is where I want to be. Honestly I'm fine. Just another new dance to learn. And frankly it's kind of a relief the sentence has finally been handed down: At least now we all know for sure.

THOMAS. You're definitely done for today. *(Wiping his tears with his sleeve, Brandt turns intently to Hannah.)*

BRANDT. But as an expert in the field of metaphysical semantics, don't you think now is a good time for a tiny little miracle? *(Hannah leans very close to Brandt, very intensely. Thomas considers the two of them very carefully.)*

HANNAH. All we can pray for today is the strength to surrender to God's will, so we might open our hearts to Him and to each other.

BRANDT. And be patient till we find each other on that distant shore?

HANNAH. *(With tremendous compassion.)* It won't be any Heaven that we've imagined. But our souls will be loosed from our bodies, all of us cradled in the arms of our Maker. This is how we surrender to the loss of our fathers and our husbands. Because God's promise is quite clear: He'll wipe away all the tears from our eyes, and there will be no more death.

THOMAS. *(His eyes locked on her.)* But you're making all of this up.

HANNAH. I beg your pardon?

THOMAS. Jesus doesn't promise anything like that in any of the gospels. You just spun all that out of whole cloth.

HANNAH. This is the way I picture it, that's all.

THOMAS. It just seems like you're taking his very specific pain and packing it away into your little box of bedtime stories.

BRANDT. It's all right. Really she's only trying to help in her way.

THOMAS. But why can't she just let you be sad about your father? Why does everything have to be an opportunity for recruitment?

HANNAH. I'm just trying to give him some kind of comfort. You care for him at least as much as I do. Surely we both want the same thing.

THOMAS. Except I think this is way more about comforting yourself. You're just playing on his pain so you can bring him around to your side.

HANNAH. I wasn't aware that we'd all chosen sides.

BRANDT. We haven't. Honestly I appreciate everything you're saying.

THOMAS. All you're doing is taking advantage of him and it sickens me.

HANNAH. *(Deeply stung.)* All I want is what's best for Brandt. And isn't it best that you call a cease-fire today, that you stop marking your territory?

BRANDT. I really don't want anybody to do anything for my benefit.

HANNAH. Because this is someone you love, and isn't he more important than any petty grievances you might have against me?

THOMAS. I'd appreciate it if you wouldn't use him as a bargaining chip.

HANNAH. I'm just saying that you have this lovely young man and you can be of real value to each other if you'd let go of all this nonsense.

THOMAS. I don't see how that has anything to do with anything.

HANNAH. This is why I told him to go after you, because I knew you could help each other, from the very first day he came here.

THOMAS. *(Stares closely at her.)* You told him to go after me? *(Hannah stares at Thomas, confused. Thomas turns to look at Brandt.)*
BRANDT. It was actually more of a request than a demand. *(Thomas is very still for a moment. He turns back to Hannah sadly.)*
THOMAS. You mean this is something you arranged for my benefit?
HANNAH. It's nothing of the sort.
THOMAS. You thought maybe I needed some kind of friendly distraction?
HANNAH. It was something I saw between you from the very first day.
THOMAS. Then you've been planning this since he walked into the house?
BRANDT. But this wasn't anything she could plan. You can't actually believe that I didn't want this more than anything.
THOMAS. *(Shifts his gaze to Brandt.)* Except what I really want to know is, did you only go after me because she asked you to?
BRANDT. But I wouldn't have had the courage otherwise. *(Thomas expels a soft breath of air. He turns to Hannah sorrowfully.)*
THOMAS. With you it's the extent that always amazes me.
HANNAH. *(Very intensely.)* Well, was I supposed to just stand idly by? Let you sit up here reading his old Bibles until you ran off again without a plan or even a map? Should I have let you walk into the ocean yourself?
THOMAS. So you were doing the Lord's work, is that it?
HANNAH. Listen, if you want to wash your hands of me, please do it already and don't drag poor Brandt into this.
THOMAS. You're the one who dragged him in. And the sad truth is he's just a strategic pawn in a much larger and far more daunting campaign.
HANNAH. And what on earth do you mean by that?
THOMAS. I'm pretty sure you thought if you could get hold of him then maybe you could have me back for good.
HANNAH. *(Taken aback a moment.)* Honestly I don't understand why I have to explain myself here.
BRANDT. *(Very quietly and simply.)* Except I guess I'd really like to know why you did it. *(They both turn to stare at Brandt. Hannah smiles at them tenderly.)*
HANNAH. Because I had faith. *(Hannah extends her arms hopefully. Thomas shakes his head slowly.)*
THOMAS. You always say it's God when it's really just you.

HANNAH. I hope you didn't come home to amass these count-less imaginary pieces of evidence against me.

THOMAS. I came home because on my birthday I stood on the shore outside Grandma's old house and I looked out at the ocean and I thought how devastating that must've been for you, how much I owe you.

HANNAH. You're a little churlish in your gratitude, do you know that?

THOMAS. And I hoped we could finally talk about how awful it still must be for you, I hoped for once maybe you wouldn't fold it all up and tuck it away with Heaven and Jesus and the pretty little angels —

HANNAH. Forgive me if I can actually find some kind of peace in this —

THOMAS. But how much peace can it actually give you when you're just terrified I'm going to follow him into the ocean all the time?

HANNAH. I don't pretend that I'm ever as enlightened as I should be —

THOMAS. When you're so desperate to keep me that you'd manipulate someone into falling in love with me and then pretend it's God's will —

BRANDT. She certainly didn't manipulate me into falling in love with you —

THOMAS. No, she arranged all this herself, and it was just to hold onto me, you're a fool if you think you matter to her one bit —

HANNAH. *(Hot with righteous anger.)* Except I really don't see how you get to judge me when you've been making the worst pos-sible life for yourself.

THOMAS. For once please don't try to make this about me.

HANNAH. Maybe you could tell me what you believe these days. What guru or cult has caught your fancy, what fortune cookie you're reading —

THOMAS. I think maybe you're making fun of me.

HANNAH. Frankly it looks to me like you're completely lost, you're just grasping hold of twigs that keep breaking off in your hands —

THOMAS. I'm certainly not going to argue with you about that.

HANNAH. Because the real question is not what your philosophy is, but how it's working for you. If it's sustaining you as you hitch-hike across the country digging ditches —

THOMAS. I freely admit that I'm making a hash of things. I'm leaving this unending stream of abandoned jobs and half-baked plans in my wake.

HANNAH. And you have to make some kind of choice in the matter. From here on out everything is written in ink, my love. You have me and you have this lovely young man who cares for you a great deal, so why can't you just let him be your way home?

THOMAS. Because you're forcing me to ricochet from place to place. And I need to be at peace with you or else I'll always be running away. So we have to be willing to ask each other the hard questions.

HANNAH. I hope I'd honestly answer any question you want to ask me. *(Thomas looks at Brandt nervously. He gulps some air before he speaks.)*

THOMAS. I'm just not sure you believe what you say you believe. *(This is all without malice. But it's clear to Brandt that something enormous is happening between them.)*

BRANDT. Are you absolutely sure you want to go down this road?

THOMAS. Pretend for one minute the rest of the world doesn't exist: It's just the three of us in this room. What do you really believe?

HANNAH. I'd like to imagine that my faith is constant even when the doors are locked and the blinds are drawn.

BRANDT. There's just no possible way that this is going to help anything.

THOMAS. It would help me enormously to know if you ever lie awake at night and wonder if you're really just talking to yourself.

HANNAH. Don't you think I question all of this every second of every day?

THOMAS. That's a little bit of a beginning at least.

HANNAH. Why should that surprise you? Belief didn't suddenly wash over me. My faith is the work of my life. I'm jealous of the people who spend an hour in church on Sunday and stroll home convinced that God's in His heaven and all's right with the world. *(Hannah is trying very hard not to get upset. Thomas shifts tensely on his feet as he watches her.)* I know I didn't become a minister because I'm so spiritually advanced. I'm here because I need it the most.

THOMAS. And do you ever wonder why you need it so desperately?

HANNAH. Believe me, I wish I was more like you. It'd be so much easier if I could just write everything off.

THOMAS. Except I think you're only holding onto your faith because you're scared of what will happen if you let go.

HANNAH. This is rapidly becoming a pointless conversation.

THOMAS. Say you fell in love with a man who walked into the ocean. *(Hannah exhales a breath of air. She turns to Brandt plaintively.)*

HANNAH. I hoped you could keep him from digging up this grave.

THOMAS. And you were lost and terrified so you reached out for these books just so you'd have something to hold onto. Who could blame you?

HANNAH. Yes, well, I'm awfully grateful for your compassion.

THOMAS. But you've been clutching them so tightly all these years, by now your knuckles are white and your palms are bleeding and where has it all gotten you anyway? You hunch over these old scraps of paper hoping against hope that they'll prove something you already know in your bones is impossible. You take innocent bystanders and you try desperately to get them to believe what you believe just so you can have some company. And you're still crying for my father as if you lost him yesterday. And you're all alone. If that's God's love then I'd say it's a pretty abusive relationship.

HANNAH. So you want to save me from all this?

THOMAS. *(With enormous tenderness.)* From where I stand, this is just how you hide from everything, this is just how you hide from me, and it breaks my heart, so all I want is to try and get through to you once and for all.

HANNAH. All I know is for three months after your father died I was so devastated I could barely move. They had to force food down my throat. I was only staying alive because I didn't want to abandon you. And when I went into labor it took two days and more than once we almost lost you. But then they put you in my arms and something hard inside me snapped and broke for good. And I felt this bottomless love for you. And I knew it had to come from God. And it brought me back to the world. Isn't that miracle enough?

THOMAS. But that's an impossible burden to place on me. I didn't ask for it and I don't want it. And anyway that's just one more story you made up, isn't it? *(Hannah stares at them both for a moment, rocked to the core.)*

HANNAH. So you think this is all just an act of will on my part?

THOMAS. If you like.

HANNAH. *(Shifts her gaze to Brandt.)* And is this what you believe about me too? That I'm just a fraud? That I'm nothing but a fool?

BRANDT. *(With enormous difficulty.)* I can't — I won't.

HANNAH. Well. My goodness. Then what kind of a creature must I be? How much damage have I done to all the people I've been trying to help? If every story I've told them is worse than useless.

THOMAS. Every story you've told me is worse than useless. And I've been your student all my life.

HANNAH. I think that's the worst thing anyone has ever said to me.

THOMAS. Believe it or not I don't mean to be cruel.

HANNAH. *(With a harsh laugh.)* All the things we never say to each other because we think they'll be too cruel. Of course in the end it usually turns out we've just been saving them for when they'll be the most cruel.

BRANDT. You both really need to stop this before it goes any further.

HANNAH. No: I think now we all need to be quite sure that we understand each other. I don't believe I've ever insisted that we follow the same path. All I've ever wanted is to try and help you.

THOMAS. But all our lives you've locked yourself away with only Jesus to keep you company and that makes it impossible for me to reach you.

HANNAH. Why don't you tell me exactly what you want from me?

THOMAS. Just to let go of something you don't need anymore. *(For a moment they're so quiet it's like they're holding their breath.)*

HANNAH. So you're asking me to give up everything I believe?

BRANDT. That's not what he means. That's not what you mean.

THOMAS. *(Nods vigorously at Brandt.)* Otherwise I don't see how we have anything to say to each other.

HANNAH. This is just another excuse for you to run away, that's all. And was anybody going to tell me? Or were you just going to sneak out in the middle of the night like always?

THOMAS. I just want you to tell the truth for once.

HANNAH. *(Turns to Brandt, sharply pained.)* I was under the impression that you were at least attempting to exert a good influence on him. That you weren't just going to send him back out into the wilderness.

BRANDT. I'm not doing everything on your behalf here.

HANNAH. *(Utterly infuriated.)* Jealousy is all this is. The jealousy of an infant. You want to know when it comes down to brass tacks that I love you more.

THOMAS. All I'm asking you to give up is a ghost story.

HANNAH. No part of you that loves me would ask me this.

THOMAS. *(Very simply and directly.)* I wish you could understand

48

that I'm only asking this out of love.

HANNAH. *(With enormous tenderness.)* Oh Thomas, there's no creature on this earth I love more than you. But the only way I could ever find the power to love you at all … it's entirely by the grace of God. There's absolutely no way for me to love you without Him. It simply isn't possible. *(As Thomas listens to her, his face slowly falls. Brandt watches them.)* And if I lose God … then I lose you a thousand times over. I'm afraid that's the only answer I can give you. *(They stare at each other. Until right now neither one of them realized it was going to come to this. Thomas shakes his head.)*

THOMAS. Then I've run out of things to say to you. *(Hannah turns to Brandt, her face stony, her voice chilled.)*

HANNAH. I asked you to keep him safe.

BRANDT. Do you actually think I meant for any of this to happen?

HANNAH. Who cares what you meant? *(Utterly controlled, Hannah gathers her books and papers together.)* We've covered everything fairly exhaustively. I'll set you free to write on your own. If you have any questions, call one of my grad students. I'll proof the manuscript once you send it to Jason. I don't think you'll need to come here for a while.

BRANDT. Are you sure that's what you want?

HANNAH. You understand I can't even look at you. *(Hannah goes out to the bedrooms. Brandt stares after her. Thomas considers Brandt very closely.)*

THOMAS. I didn't realize she had her hooks in you that far.

BRANDT. *(A weak smile.)* You can't be the servant of two masters. I'm pretty sure that's the appropriate verse.

THOMAS. Did she make you give her a daily report on my mental health?

BRANDT. You know it was only because she's so worried about you.

THOMAS. Did you have to keep her up to date on my progress?

BRANDT. She never asked me about anything private.

THOMAS. I guess I'm curious to what extent I've been played for a fool. *(Brandt stares at his feet for a moment before he speaks.)*

BRANDT. I should've told you a long time ago. It's just, this thing we all constructed, it seemed so fragile, I didn't even want to breathe for fear of wrecking it. I don't mean that as an excuse.

THOMAS. In the end I guess you were always more hers than mine.

BRANDT. I wish you wouldn't make us all choose sides.

THOMAS. All I'm saying is, I'm sure you understand, right now I need my life to be as much untied from hers as possible.

BRANDT. But listen, nothing ever comes to you entirely clean, and if you walk away from everything once it gets a little tarnished, you'll always be walking away. And you can't possibly have any doubts about how much I want to keep you.

THOMAS. I just need some time to think hard about this is all.

BRANDT. I wonder if you've already decided what you're going to do and you're just picking this fight to make things easier for yourself. *(Thomas stares at Brandt across the length of the room for a moment.)*

THOMAS. I want to take into account how terrible things are for you right now. You've got more than enough on your plate and I have no intention of leaving you in the lurch.

BRANDT. So you'd stick around out of pity for me?

THOMAS. This isn't about pity.

BRANDT. Hell, I don't care if that's what it is. Where you're concerned I'm not all that proud.

THOMAS. What I'm saying is I'm not going to abandon you right now.

BRANDT. *(Takes a deep breath.)* Here's the problem: What's going on for me will only get more impossible. Long before it ends, he won't be able to dress himself, his fingers won't be able to tie his own shoes.

THOMAS. Which is exactly why I want to make sure you're taken care of.

BRANDT. It's probably going to drag on for years and if you're not in it for the long haul then I can't use you. On top of everything else I can't always be wondering if you've got one eye on the door.

THOMAS. That's the last thing I want too.

BRANDT. Then I need you to be hard about this. Because every day you stay with me I'm only gonna get more tied up in you. So if you really don't want to be here anymore then make a break for it now before I'm too far gone. *(Thomas' face slowly changes. Brandt cups his face in his hands.)*

THOMAS. We knew this probably wouldn't be forever.

BRANDT. You never made me any promises.

THOMAS. At least this way you've only lost a month or two.

BRANDT. Except I've been walking around building a home for us in my head. There's fifty years ahead of us we've both lost now.

THOMAS. Don't say that. It isn't even true.

BRANDT. Hey, listen, I fully intend to take you at your word, so I'm only gonna ask once, but are you sure this is what you want?

Because otherwise I'll look back and wonder if I should've fought harder.

THOMAS. *(As gently as possible.)* In the end you're just not what I'm chasing. *(Brandt toes the floorboards with his shoe. His voice is low.)*

BRANDT. Well, then: You can't argue when there's real disagreement.

THOMAS. So what are we supposed to do now?

BRANDT. *(Upset but very controlled.)* Are you asking for my help in ending this well? Because that's incomprehensible to me. Really I don't understand the question.

THOMAS. You know that's not what I mean.

BRANDT. Because I'm going to be angry at you for a very long time. Those are actually my only plans at the moment if you want the truth.

THOMAS. I understand you must think very little of me.

BRANDT. *(With a surge of pain.)* I think you folded up like a card table the second something was genuinely asked of you, so I think absolutely nothing of you.

THOMAS. *(With enormous tenderness.)* If you think for a second that I was just playing here — don't you know how much I wanted this to be the place I finally landed? *(Brandt's anger burns out of him and he just looks very sad and tired.)*

BRANDT. So where do you think you'll go?

THOMAS. It's not like I've had much time to make plans.

BRANDT. I know one thing about you, you've always got an escape route.

THOMAS. My buddy Roger has a farm up in Putnam, maybe I can pick up some work with him. I've got a buddy who's a park ranger in Taos. Or maybe I really will just get lost for a while.

BRANDT. Burn all the cash in your wallet, take off for parts unknown?

THOMAS. Something like that. Are you worried about me like my mother is? Think I'm digging myself an early grave?

BRANDT. I'm more worried you'll live till you're a hundred and you'll never figure out what you're chasing.

THOMAS. I know for a fact that everything is gonna come around for you.

BRANDT. *(Recites lightly from memory.)* "These all died in faith, not having received the promises, but having seen them afar off were assured of them, embraced them, and confessed that they were strangers and pilgrims on this earth."

THOMAS. Boy, my mother really did get her hooks in you, didn't she?

BRANDT. *(Smiles slightly.)* That was my confirmation reading. All those people wandering in the desert forty years, most of them died still having faith because they could see their home way in the distance. So I guess all we get is just this little glimpse of each other. *(Brandt starts to pack up his knapsack. Thomas watches him.)*

THOMAS. You don't have to go just yet.

BRANDT. In case you've forgotten I've been kicked out of your house.

THOMAS. She'll forgive you. It's another requirement of the uniform.

BRANDT. Actually I'd like to get out of here myself if that's okay.

THOMAS. Whatever you want. *(Brandt heads out. On the way there he stops and turns back to Thomas.)*

BRANDT. The one way your mother really did get her hooks in me, I found it impossible not to believe there was some kind of benevolent force in the universe when you were standing next to me.

THOMAS. Take care of yourself. *(Brandt goes out. Thomas sits alone on the floor. He starts to pack his things. He picks up the model airplane and considers it closely. He sends it flying across the room. The lights fade.)*

Scene 3

Noon on a Friday in February. Snow is falling steadily outside. Hannah stares out the windows. It's the first time that we've seen her dressed in her full robes. Tentatively Brandt steps into the room and knocks lightly on the side of the door. He wears a dark suit. Hannah turns to see him.

HANNAH. Are you waiting for me?

BRANDT. We have about five more minutes.

HANNAH. How is your mother holding up?

BRANDT. My aunts have taken her under their wing. They're gossiping about everyone else at the funeral. This guy married his secretary who turned out to be a kleptomaniac, that lady had both her kneecaps replaced. It's torture for her but at least it's distracting.

HANNAH. And how are you?

BRANDT. *(As neutrally as possible.)* It's like the roof came off the house.

HANNAH. If it's all right I thought I'd start with the prayer you liked so much when you were a boy. Then I can talk about his thirty years at his job, how much he loved you and your mother. The clippings you sent me were very helpful.

BRANDT. It was over so much faster than we expected. We'd only had that one conversation months ago about what he wanted. I wouldn't have called you but I don't know anyone else.

HANNAH. *(Extends her arms.)* This is what I do.

BRANDT. Is there anything else you need from me?

HANNAH. Did you decide if you're going to speak?

BRANDT. I remembered something when I was walking over here this morning. Christmas Eve every year when I was little my dad would read "A Visit from St. Nicholas" and act it out for me. *(Brandt leans against the table. Hannah nods, smiling slightly.)* One year, I was six or seven, he got to the part about tearing open the shutters and throwing up the sash, so he threw back the curtains and at that exact moment it started to snow. I couldn't tell who made that happen: my father or Santa Claus or God.

HANNAH. That's a lovely story.

BRANDT. *(Toes the floor with his shoe.)* I wasn't sure I wanted to see you again.

HANNAH. I don't think I've ever been as far away from God as I was with you. I'll be trying to repay those damages till the day I die.

BRANDT. I know everything you did was because you love Thomas so much. *(Hannah looks at her hands. It costs her enormously to ask this.)*

HANNAH. If you knew where he was, would you tell me?

BRANDT. I don't know where he is. *(Hannah lets this wash over her for a moment before she speaks again.)*

HANNAH. I read your draft of our book. I have a number of corrections but for the most part I think we're in very good shape.

BRANDT. I didn't know what to say in the afterword. If you think this was the first gospel. You never said what you decided.

HANNAH. Say I don't think it matters one way or the other anymore. It's just one more voice crying out in the wilderness, trying to make sense of this extraordinary life.

BRANDT. The last few hours with my father, when they knew it was all over, they were pumping the morphine through him and it was like I could see each cell in his body shuddering and dying one by one. And I suddenly felt a kind of love I'd never felt before: It was hard and pitiless as steel. And I held his hand till he wasn't there anymore. And I thought this must be what you meant by God's love.

HANNAH. I think that's what it might be.

BRANDT. But what's the use of loving people so strongly and passionately when in the end it isn't nearly enough to save them?

HANNAH. I don't know. But I believe it's the closest we ever get to understanding the way God loves us.

BRANDT. The truth is, no matter how hard I try I can't see God anywhere. All I can see is the empty space where He's supposed to be. I can't tell if that's the beginning of faith or the end of it. *(Hannah stares out the window at the snow for a moment. Then she turns and extends her arms to Brandt.)*

HANNAH. Let's bury our dead.

End of Play

PROPERTY LIST

Books, Bibles
Pens, papers
Package of papers
Letter opener
Folder
Manuscript
Knapsack
Porcupine quills
Keys
Toolbox, tool belt
Purse, scarf
Knapsack with x-rays
Box of model airplanes
Dead leaves
Thai takeout dinner
Bottle of wine, glasses
Notebooks
Telescope
Picnic blanket

Rain